The Very Christmas Day

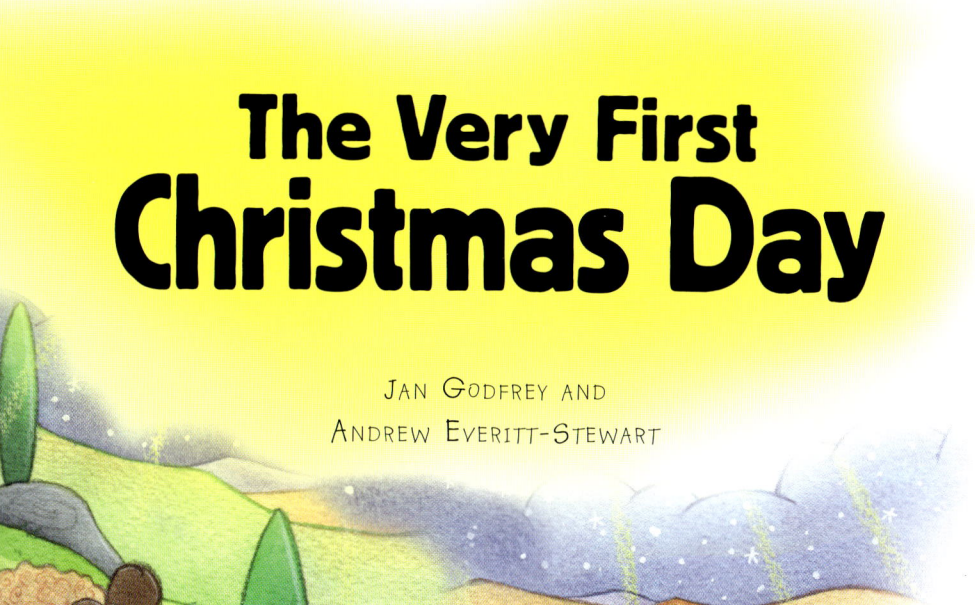

The Very First Christmas Day

Jan Godfrey and
Andrew Everitt-Stewart

Along the road, along the road, to the very first Christmas day, Mary had a surprise visitor – a beautiful angel!

'Hello, Mary,' said the angel. 'God has chosen you to do something very special. You are going to have a baby son, the son of God Himself. Name him Jesus – because he is going to save his people. Don't be afraid.'

Mary was afraid, very, VERY afraid, but she wanted to do as God told her.

'But how will this happen?' Mary wondered. 'I am not even married.'

'Nothing is too hard for God,' said the angel.

Mary looked and listened, she listened and she looked. Then the beautiful angel went away.

Along the road, along the road, to the very first Christmas day, Mary hurried to a town in the hills, to see her cousin Elizabeth.

'I'm so happy!' said Mary. 'God has done something wonderful! I am going to be a mother, the mother of a baby son, God's own son!'

Elizabeth looked and listened, she listened and she looked.
Then with Mary she praised God for the wonderful news.

Along the road, along the road, to the very first Christmas day, Mary travelled to the little town of Bethlehem with good, kind Joseph at her side.

'We have to be counted,' said Joseph.
'We have to go to Bethlehem.'

Mary looked and listened, she listened and she looked. She saw the twinkling stars along the rocky roads, winding between the trees and houses. She heard the donkey's hooves, clip-clop, clip-clop, all the way to Bethlehem.

Along the road, along the road, to the very first Christmas day, Mary knew that soon her baby son would be born.

Mary looked and listened, she listened and she looked. She saw many people, she saw many donkeys and she heard many voices, all the way to Bethlehem.

Along the road, along the road, to the very first Christmas day, Mary and Joseph knocked at doors, hoping for somewhere to stay.

Mary looked and listened, she listened and she looked. But every inn was full and every room was taken.

Knock! Knock! 'No room!'

Knock! Knock! 'No room, no room!'

Then Joseph knocked at one more door...

'There aren't any rooms, but you can rest out with the animals, here in Bethlehem.'

In Bethlehem, that holy night, on the very first Christmas day, Mary's baby son was born.

Mary looked and listened, she listened and she looked. She saw the ox and donkey, she saw the starry skies. She held her baby, Jesus, and she heard his little cries. She wrapped him up to keep him warm, and laid him in a manger.

Along the road, out on the hills, on the very first Christmas day, shepherds huddling with their sheep saw a bright and shining light!

They looked and listened, they listened and they looked. They saw an angel, they heard good news!

'Don't be afraid,' said the angel. 'God's son, Jesus Christ, is born in Bethlehem today!'

The shepherds saw more angels filling the sky. They saw a dazzling, heavenly light. They saw a great host of angels and they heard songs of praise to God.

Along the road, above the hills,
on the very first Christmas day,
the angels sang, 'Glory to God
and peace to all the earth.'

The shepherds looked and listened, they listened and they looked.
They saw their sheep out on the hills, they saw the starry skies.
They hurried down to Bethlehem where Jesus was born that night.

Along the road, along the road, on the very first Christmas day, the shepherds reached the stable and found a baby in a manger.

The shepherds looked and listened, they listened and they looked. They saw the baby sleeping in the bed Mary had made for him.

They heard the snuffly animals next to the crowded inn. Then they told their story of the angels in the sky.

Mary listened to the shepherds. Her heart was full of joy. Then the shepherds told everyone they met what they had seen and heard.

Along the road, along the road and very far away, some wise men looked and listened, they listened and they looked. They saw a new star in the sky. They saw their camels waiting.

'A baby King has been born!' they said.
'We must go and find him.'
'We must worship him,' they said.
'We must take gifts to the baby King.'

Along the road, a long, long road, the road to find the King, the wise men followed the star while they looked and listened, they listened and they looked.

'Look at the star!'

'It's right over that house!'

'It's right over that house in Bethlehem!'

Along the road, with gifts of love, along the road to worship him, the wise men left their camels and went into the little house.

They looked and listened, they listened and they looked. They saw the little Jesus. They saw his mother Mary. They knelt down and worshipped him with their gifts – gold, sweet-smelling frankincense and myrrh – fit for a King, a heavenly, human *baby* King.

Along the road, the wise men rode, along the road and home again.
'We've seen the King, the son of God.'
'We've knelt and offered gifts to him.'
'We've worshipped Jesus,' the wise men said.

'We've worshipped Christ the King.'

They had looked and listened, they'd listened and they'd looked. They had seen the star and followed. They'd worshipped Christ, the baby King.

Now the world was different. It had Jesus, and its very first Christmas day.

If you would like to read this story in a Bible,
you will find it in Luke's Gospel chapter 1,
verses 26-56 and chapter 2 verses 1-21;
and Matthew's Gospel, chapter 2 verses 1-23.

First edition 2008 under the title 'The Road to Christmas Day'
This revised edition 2015

Copyright © 2015 Anno Domini Publishing
www.ad-publishing.com

Text copyright © 2015 Jan Godfrey
Illustrations copyright © 2015 Andrew Everitt-Stewart

All rights reserved

Printed and bound in Singapore

Published 2015 by CWR, Waverley Abbey House, Waverley Lane, Farnham, Surrey, GU9 8EP, UK.
Registered Charity No. 294387. Registered Limited Company No. 1990308.
For a list of National Distributors, visit www.cwr.org.uk/distributors